HEAVEN'S COURTROOM

PASTOR DR. CLAUDINE BENJAMIN

For more information or to book an event, contact:
inspiredtowinsouls@gmail.com

Published by:

Editor: Cleveland O. McLeish (Author C. Orville McLeish)

ISBN: 978-1-965635-73-5 (paperback)

Scripture quotations marked "KJV" are taken from the Holy Bible, King James Version (Public Domain).

ABOUT THE AUTHOR

Pastor Claudine Benjamin is a prophetic voice and teacher of the Word whose ministry carries a strong emphasis on revival, intercession, and the urgency of preparing the bride of Christ for His return. With a heart of compassion and a mandate of truth, she has devoted her life to preaching the gospel, equipping believers, and raising a generation who understand their identity, authority, and eternal destiny in Christ.

Her writings, like her preaching, are marked by depth, clarity, and urgency. She carries a passion to unveil the realities of heaven and expose the strategies of the enemy, so that the church may walk in victory and holiness.

In The Courtroom in Heaven, Pastor Benjamin draws from Scripture and the leading of the Holy Spirit to reveal the divine legal system that governs heaven and earth. Through practical insight and prophetic revelation, she equips believers to silence the accuser, present their case before God, and enforce heaven's verdicts on earth.

She has authored multiple works focused on spiritual growth, healing, resilience, and evangelism. Her books carry a consistent theme: that God's people are not called to merely survive but to live victoriously, fulfilling the great commission with passion and fire.

When she is not writing or ministering, Pastor Benjamin mentors, counsels, and encourages individuals to embrace their God-given purpose. She remains committed to building lives, strengthening the church, and pointing souls to the eternal hope found in Jesus Christ.

DEDICATION

To the Righteous Judge of all the earth, whose throne is established in justice and truth, and to Jesus Christ, my Advocate, who pleads my case daily with the evidence of His blood.

This work is dedicated to every believer who has felt the sting of the accuser's voice, yet will discover through these pages that the verdict is already in their favor. May you rise, plead your case with boldness, and walk in the victory of heaven's courtroom.

I also dedicate this book to future generations—sons and daughters who will learn to silence the enemy, not with fear but with the Word, the blood, and their testimony.

ACKNOWLEDGMENT

I humbly thank my heavenly Father for the revelation, strength, and wisdom to write this book. Without His Spirit's leading, the courtroom of heaven would have remained a mystery to me.

To my Lord and Savior Jesus Christ—thank You for being my constant Defender, Intercessor, and Advocate who never loses a case.

To the Holy Spirit—thank You for being the faithful Witness who convicts, comforts, and confirms every truth written here.

I extend heartfelt gratitude to my family, loved ones, and church community who encouraged me, prayed for me, and carried me through this assignment with unwavering love.

Finally, I acknowledge every reader of this book. You are not just holding a manuscript—you are holding a legal manual of victory. My prayer is that these pages ignite boldness, remove fear, and empower you to live as more than conquerors in Christ.

TABLE OF CONTENTS

Part IV

Walking in Victory After the Verdict

INTRODUCTION

HEAVEN'S COURTROOM

In the scriptures, God often reveals His nature and dealings with humanity through familiar earthly images. One of the most sobering and majestic is that of a courtroom. The Bible speaks of God as the righteous Judge who sits enthroned in heaven, with angels as witnesses, books of record opened, and verdicts rendered that determine eternal destinies. Heaven's courtroom is not a metaphor of imagination; it is a divine reality where the justice, holiness, and authority of almighty God are displayed without compromise.

When we think of a courtroom on earth, we picture a judge presiding, lawyers presenting cases, evidence being examined, and a final verdict being pronounced. In heaven's courtroom, these elements take on eternal weight. God is the ultimate Judge, Christ is our Advocate (**see 1 John 2:1**), and Satan stands as the accuser of the brethren (**see Revelation 12:10**). The evidence presented is the record of our lives, the words we have spoken, and the deeds we have done (**see Ecclesiastes 12:14, Matthew 12:36**). The stakes are higher than any earthly trial—for the outcome determines eternal life or eternal separation from God.

This heavenly courtroom reminds us that life is not random, nor are our actions without accountability. Every prayer, sin, act of obedience, rejection of God's call—nothing escapes the record of the Judge of all the earth. Yet, for the believer, this sobering reality is also our greatest comfort. Jesus Christ, our Defender, has already secured our acquittal through His blood shed on Calvary. In heaven's courtroom, mercy and truth meet, righteousness and peace kiss each other (**see Psalm 85:10**).

As we enter this study, we must understand that heaven's courtroom is not merely about the fear of judgment but also about the assurance of redemption. It is the place where justice is satisfied, sin is confronted, the guilty are condemned, and the repentant are pardoned. It is where God's sovereignty over history and humanity is established, and where eternity is decided.

This introduction sets the stage for teaching on spiritual warfare, intercession, accountability, and the eternal perspective of God's justice.

THE REALITY OF THE COURTROOM IN HEAVEN

The Bible presents heaven not only as a place of worship, glory, and eternal dwelling but also as a place of government and judgment. One of the clearest pictures of this is heaven as a courtroom. This is where God, the righteous Judge, sits enthroned, where cases are presented, accusations are heard, and verdicts are rendered. Unlike earthly courts, heaven's courtroom is flawless—there is no corruption, no miscarriage of justice, and no hidden evidence. Every word, thought, and deed is fully known and weighed by the God who sees all (**see Hebrews 4:13**).

Daniel, in his vision, saw this courtroom in motion:

> **"I beheld till the thrones were cast down, and the Ancient of days did sit… the judgment was set, and the books were opened." (Daniel 7:9–10 - KJV).**

This is not imagination—it is revelation. The books of record are real, the Judge is real, and the trials are ongoing.

THE JUDGE: GOD ALMIGHTY

At the center of heaven's courtroom is God Himself. Scripture calls Him the **"Judge of all the earth" (see Genesis 18:25)**. His judgment is final, His decrees unshakable, and His authority unquestioned. Unlike human judges, God is not swayed by bribes, emotions, or flawed evidence. His judgments are always righteous and true.

The psalmist declares: **"For the Lord is our judge, the Lord is our lawgiver, the Lord is our king; he will save us." (Isaiah 33:22 - KJV).** Notice the completeness: God is the one who gives the law, judges by it, and reigns as sovereign over its outcome.

THE ADVOCATE: JESUS CHRIST

No courtroom would be complete without legal representation, and in heaven's courtroom, Jesus Christ Himself stands as our Advocate. The apostle John reassures us:

> **"…if any man sin, we have an advocate with the Father, Jesus Christ the righteous." (1 John 2:1 - KJV).**

13

An advocate is one who pleads on behalf of another. Christ's advocacy is not built on human reasoning but on His finished work at Calvary. His blood speaks louder than the accusations of the enemy (**see Hebrews 12:24**). When Satan points out our sins, Jesus points to His cross. When the accuser shouts condemnation, Jesus presents the evidence of His sacrifice.

In heaven's courtroom, our defense is not our good works, our ministry, or our reputation. Our defense is Christ alone.

THE ACCUSER: SATAN

Every courtroom has a prosecuting voice, and in heaven's courtroom, that role is played by Satan. **Revelation 12:10** calls him **"the accuser of our brethren… which accused them before our God day and night." (KJV).**

Satan's strategy is consistent: he digs up our failures, magnifies our weaknesses, and presents them as evidence to disqualify us from God's presence. His accusations are not without foundation—many times they are based on real sins and shortcomings. Yet his goal is not justice but condemnation. He seeks to destroy, not restore.

This is why the believer must cling to Christ's advocacy. Without the blood of Jesus, Satan's accusations would stand, and we would be found guilty. But through Christ, the verdict is reversed: the guilty are pardoned, and the condemned are justified.

THE WITNESSES: ANGELS AND THE CLOUD OF SAINTS

A courtroom requires witnesses. In heaven, these are both angelic and human. **Hebrews 12:1** describes a **"great...cloud of witnesses" (KJV)**—the saints who have gone before us, testifying to the faithfulness of God. Angels also play a role, both observing and testifying to the actions of men (**see 1 Corinthians 4:9**).

This reminds us that our lives are not lived in secret. Every choice, word, and action is recorded and witnessed. This should humble us, but also encourage us: the righteous deeds done in secret are also remembered and testified to in heaven's courtroom.

THE EVIDENCE: THE BOOKS

Daniel saw the books opened. Revelation 20:12 confirms it:

> **"And I saw the dead, small and great, stand before God; and the books were opened... and the dead were judged out of those things which were written in the books, according to their works." (KJV).**

The evidence presented in heaven's courtroom is not circumstantial—it is written. The record of every action, every intention, every prayer, and every sin is kept. But there is another book—the Book of Life. All who have put their trust in Christ have their names written there, and that book outweighs every other. If your name is found in the Book of Life, the verdict is eternal salvation (**see Revelation 20:15**).

THE VERDICT: ETERNAL DESTINY

In heaven's courtroom, there is no hung jury, no mistrial, no appeal. The verdict is final, and it is eternal. To the unrepentant, the sentence is separation from God forever in the lake of fire. To the redeemed, the verdict is "not guilty"—pardoned and welcomed into eternal fellowship with God.

This is why the courtroom of heaven is both terrifying and comforting. Terrifying to those who reject Christ, but comforting to those who trust Him as their Advocate.

LIVING WITH HEAVEN'S COURTROOM IN MIND

Understanding heaven's courtroom should change how we live. We are reminded that:

1. **Nothing is hidden** – our lives are an open book before God.

2. **Christ is our only defense** – no religious effort or moral achievement can acquit us.

3. **The enemy is relentless** – Satan accuses day and night, but we overcome him **"by the blood of the Lamb, and by the word of (our) testimony." (Revelation 12:11 - KJV).**

4. **The verdict is eternal** – decisions made on earth determine eternity in heaven.

PRAYER

Righteous Judge of all the earth, I acknowledge Your throne, Your justice, and Your authority. Thank You for appointing Jesus Christ as my Advocate, whose blood speaks for me when the accuser rises against me. Help me to live daily with the awareness of heaven's courtroom, walking in holiness, humility, and trust in Your mercy. May my name remain in the Book of Life, and may my life bear witness to Your truth until the day I stand before You. Amen.

PART I

ENTERING THE COURTROOM

CHAPTER 1

THE REALITY OF HEAVEN'S COURTROOM

T he scriptures reveal that heaven is not only a place of worship, angelic activity, and eternal glory, but it is also a courtroom where divine legal proceedings take place. God, who is the Righteous Judge, rules from His throne. The Bible paints a vivid picture of this heavenly court, where cases are heard, verdicts are rendered, and eternal destinies are determined.

THE JUDGE OF ALL THE EARTH

Abraham, in interceding for Sodom, appealed to God's justice:

"Shall not the Judge of all the earth do right?" (Genesis 18:25, KJV).

This introduces us to God as the Judge, seated upon His throne, presiding with justice, mercy, and truth. Unlike earthly courts, which can be corrupted by bribes or partiality, heaven's courtroom operates under the unshakable foundation of righteousness and holiness.

THE ASSEMBLY OF THE COURT

The prophet Daniel was given a vision of the heavenly court:

> **"I beheld till the thrones were cast down, and the Ancient of days did sit… his throne was like the fiery flame… The judgment was set, and the books were opened." (Daniel 7:9–10, KJV).**

Here we see a divine courtroom scene: thrones, the Judge, innumerable angels, and books that contain records of human deeds. These books represent evidence—nothing is hidden before God's eyes. Every thought, word, and action is weighed.

THE REALITY OF LEGAL PROCEEDINGS

Job's experience unveils another glimpse into this heavenly courtroom. The Bible says:

> **"Now there was a day when the sons of God came to present themselves before the Lord, and Satan came also among them." (Job 1:6, KJV).**

This scene reveals that heaven's courtroom entertains petitions and accusations. Satan, the adversary, acts as the accuser, bringing charges against believers. Yet, this also shows us that no accusation can proceed without God's permission.

THE WITNESS OF SCRIPTURE

The New Testament affirms this courtroom reality:

"But ye are come unto mount Sion, and unto the city of the living God, the heavenly Jerusalem… to God the Judge of all, and to the spirits of just men made perfect." (Hebrews 12:22–23, KJV).

Notice that the believer enters into the presence of God as Judge, not only as Father and Savior. This means that, as children of God, we must understand our legal standing before Him.

WHY THE COURTROOM MATTERS FOR BELIEVERS

Many Christians focus only on God as Father or Shepherd, but neglect to recognize His role as Judge. In the courtroom of heaven:

- Accusations are brought (**see Revelation 12:10**).
- Evidence is presented (**see Ecclesiastes 12:14**).
- Verdicts are issued (**see Psalm 9:7–8**).
- Sentences are executed (**see Romans 2:5–6**).

Understanding this gives us confidence in prayer. When we intercede, we are not merely begging for mercy but also presenting legal petitions before the Righteous Judge who responds to His Word.

KEY SCRIPTURES

- Genesis 18:25
- Daniel 7:9–10
- Job 1:6
- Hebrews 12:22–23
- Revelation 12:10
- Ecclesiastes 12:14

- Psalm 9:7–8
- Romans 2:5–6

CHAPTER 2

GOD THE JUDGE OF ALL THE EARTH

W hen Abraham stood before the Lord to intercede for the city of Sodom, he raised one of the most profound questions ever spoken:

"That be far from thee to do after this manner, to slay the righteous with the wicked... Shall not the Judge of all the earth do right?" (Genesis 18:25, KJV).

This declaration acknowledges God as Judge—a role inseparable from His divine character. To truly understand the heavenly courtroom, we must grasp who God is in His judicial authority.

THE NATURE OF GOD AS JUDGE

God is not merely a judge by title—He embodies justice itself. Unlike earthly judges, He cannot be swayed, corrupted, or misled. His judgments are perfect because His nature is perfect.

- "He is the Rock, his work is perfect: for all his ways are judgment: a God of truth and without iniquity, just and right is he." (Deuteronomy 32:4, KJV).

- "For the LORD is our judge, the LORD is our lawgiver, the LORD is our king; he will save us." (Isaiah 33:22, KJV).

Here we see God in a threefold role: Judge (who decides), Lawgiver (who sets the standard), and King (who enforces the verdict). This is the divine order of the courtroom of heaven.

THE THRONE OF JUDGMENT

The Psalms often describe God as seated upon a throne of justice:

"But the LORD shall endure for ever: he hath prepared his throne for judgment. And he shall judge the world in righteousness, he shall minister judgment to the people in uprightness." (Psalm 9:7–8, KJV).

The throne of God is not merely symbolic. It represents His supreme authority and His right to govern the universe. Every soul—whether righteous or wicked—will one day stand before Him.

THE STANDARD OF JUDGMENT

God's judgments are based on His unchanging Word. What He has spoken becomes the standard by which humanity is measured.

"For God shall bring every work into judgment, with every secret thing, whether it be good, or whether it be evil." (Ecclesiastes 12:14, KJV).

"So then every one of us shall give account of himself to God." (Romans 14:12, KJV).

Nothing escapes His sight, and nothing is exempt from His judgment. His standard is not shifting human opinion but His eternal truth.

GOD AS RIGHTEOUS DEFENDER

For believers, the truth that God is Judge should not inspire terror, but confidence. Why? Because the Judge Himself is also our Defender.

"He shall judge the poor of the people, he shall save the children of the needy, and shall break in pieces the oppressor." (Psalm 72:4, KJV).

The same Judge who weighs our deeds is also the One who delivers us from the accusations of the enemy. His verdict is always for the cause of righteousness and against the cause of evil.

THE FINAL JUDGMENT

The ultimate courtroom session is yet to come, when all nations will stand before Him.

"And I saw a great white throne, and him that sat on it… and the dead were judged out of those things which were

written in the books, according to their works."
(Revelation 20:11–12, KJV).

This moment underscores the seriousness of God's role as Judge. Every verdict He issues is eternal—there is no appeal beyond His throne.

APPLICATION: APPROACHING THE JUDGE WITH CONFIDENCE

Understanding God as Judge helps us approach Him rightly. It means:

- We can come boldly to His throne (**see Hebrews 4:16**).

- We can present our petitions in faith, knowing He is just (**see 1 John 1:9**).

- We can rest assured that injustice will never prevail against righteousness.

The believer's confidence lies in the fact that God, the Judge of all the earth, always does what is right.

KEY SCRIPTURES

- Genesis 18:25
- Deuteronomy 32:4
- Isaiah 33:22
- Psalm 9:7–8
- Ecclesiastes 12:14
- Romans 14:12

- Psalm 72:4
- Revelation 20:11–12
- Hebrews 4:16
- 1 John 1:9

CHAPTER 3

THE ACCUSER OF THE BRETHREN

E very courtroom has a prosecutor—the one who brings charges against the accused. In the heavenly courtroom, that role is filled by none other than Satan, the adversary of God's people. The scriptures call him "the accuser of our brethren" (**see Revelation 12:10**). Understanding his role helps us know both the seriousness of his accusations and the power we have through Christ to overcome them.

SATAN THE ADVERSARY

The very name "Satan" means adversary or one who resists. From the beginning, he has opposed the purposes of God and the people of God. He operates in the courtroom of heaven as the accuser, attempting to discredit believers before the Judge.

> **"Now there was a day when the sons of God came to present themselves before the LORD, and Satan came also among them." (Job 1:6, KJV).**

"And the Lord said unto Satan, Whence comest thou? Then Satan answered the Lord, and said, From going to and fro in the earth, and from walking up and down in it." (Job 1:7, KJV).

Here we see Satan entering the courtroom to bring accusations against Job. He prowls the earth, gathering "evidence," and then seeks to present it before God.

THE NATURE OF HIS ACCUSATIONS

Satan's accusations are both relentless and strategic. He seeks to exploit human weakness, magnify failures, and distort truth.

"And he shewed me Joshua the high priest standing before the angel of the LORD, and Satan standing at his right hand to resist him." (Zechariah 3:1, KJV).

Notice that Satan stands ready to resist—always seeking grounds to accuse. He does not invent God's laws; he simply seeks to twist them into a case against the saints.

CONTINUOUS ACCUSATION

Unlike earthly prosecutors who work on limited cases, Satan accuses day and night.

"For the accuser of our brethren is cast down, which accused them before our God day and night." (Revelation 12:10, KJV).

This reveals both his persistence and his hatred for God's children. Yet the scripture does not end with the accuser—it continues with the victory of the saints.

THE ACCUSER VS. THE ADVOCATE

The accusations of Satan are serious, but they do not stand uncontested. For every prosecutor, there must be a defense attorney. Jesus Christ is that Advocate.

> **"My little children, these things write I unto you, that ye sin not. And if any man sin, we have an advocate with the Father, Jesus Christ the righteous." (1 John 2:1, KJV).**

Satan presents the charges; Christ presents the defense. Satan points to guilt; Christ points to the blood. Satan demands judgment; Christ provides justification.

THE BASIS OF HIS DEFEAT

The accuser does not win in the heavenly courtroom. Believers are given the legal right to overcome him through two things:

> **"And they overcame him by the blood of the Lamb, and by the word of their testimony; and they loved not their lives unto the death." (Revelation 12:11, KJV).**

1. **The Blood of the Lamb** – The blood of Jesus is the ultimate evidence that cancels every accusation.

2. **The Word of Testimony** – Our confession of faith and alignment with God's Word stands as a testimony in court.

When these two are presented, the accuser is silenced.

APPLICATION: RECOGNIZING THE ENEMY'S STRATEGY

The enemy often whispers condemnation to the believer's mind, echoing the same accusations he brings before God. Understanding that his role is to accuse helps us discern the difference between conviction from the Holy Spirit and condemnation from Satan.

- Conviction leads to repentance and restoration.
- Condemnation leads to guilt, shame, and paralysis.

As children of God, we must not agree with the accuser's voice. Instead, we must stand on the finished work of Christ, declaring His blood as our defense.

Key Scriptures

- Revelation 12:10–11
- Job 1:6–7
- Zechariah 3:1
- 1 John 2:1
- Romans 8:33–34

CHAPTER 4

THE ADVOCATE: JESUS CHRIST THE RIGHTEOUS

In every courtroom, when accusations are raised, the accused needs a defense attorney—one who speaks on their behalf, presents their case, and secures their freedom. In the courtroom of heaven, that Advocate is none other than Jesus Christ the Righteous.

John declares:

> **"My little children, these things write I unto you, that ye sin not. And if any man sin, we have an advocate with the Father, Jesus Christ the righteous." (1 John 2:1, KJV).**

The term "advocate" in Greek is parakletos, meaning *"one who is called to stand beside."* It is a legal word, describing a lawyer or mediator who pleads a case. Jesus does not merely sympathize with us; He legally defends us before the Father.

JESUS, OUR MEDIATOR

Paul confirms this truth when he writes:

> **"For there is one God, and one mediator between God and men, the man Christ Jesus." (1 Timothy 2:5, KJV).**

This shows that Jesus stands in the gap, reconciling humanity with God. He bridges the separation caused by sin, ensuring that no accusation can separate us from the love of God.

THE RIGHTEOUS BASIS OF HIS ADVOCACY

Unlike earthly lawyers, Jesus does not defend us on the basis of false claims or insufficient evidence. He defends us on the solid foundation of His righteousness and His finished work at Calvary.

> **"Who is he that condemneth? It is Christ that died, yea rather, that is risen again, who is even at the right hand of God, who also maketh intercession for us." (Romans 8:34, KJV).**

Our defense is not rooted in our innocence, but in His sacrifice. Jesus does not say, *"They never sinned."* Instead, He declares, *"Their sins are paid in full by My blood."*

THE POWER OF HIS BLOOD AS EVIDENCE

The blood of Jesus is the most powerful evidence in the courtroom of heaven. It speaks louder than every accusation.

> **"And to Jesus the mediator of the new covenant, and to the blood of sprinkling, that speaketh better things than that of Abel." (Hebrews 12:24, KJV).**

Abel's blood cried out for vengeance (**see Genesis 4:10**), but Jesus' blood cries out for mercy, forgiveness, and justification. Each drop testifies that the price for sin has been satisfied.

HIS ONGOING INTERCESSION

Jesus does not only advocate for us once—He continually intercedes for His people.

> **"Wherefore he is able also to save them to the uttermost that come unto God by him, seeing he ever liveth to make intercession for them." (Hebrews 7:25, KJV).**

Day after day, Jesus presents His finished work before the Father. Every time the enemy raises a charge, Jesus points to the cross, silencing the accuser with His eternal sacrifice.

OUR CONFIDENCE BEFORE THE JUDGE

Because Jesus is our Advocate, we can come into the courtroom with boldness, not fear.

> **"Let us therefore come boldly unto the throne of grace, that we may obtain mercy, and find grace to help in time of need." (Hebrews 4:16, KJV).**

We are not left to defend ourselves. The greatest defense attorney in all eternity stands by our side, declaring us justified, redeemed, and reconciled to God.

APPLICATION: LIVING WITH ASSURANCE

Knowing Jesus as our Advocate changes how we walk with God:

- We approach prayer with confidence, not shame.
- We reject condemnation, knowing our defense is secure.
- We live in gratitude, honoring the One who stands for us.

When Satan accuses, when conscience condemns, and when the world rejects, we can rest in the assurance that Jesus Christ the Righteous pleads our case and never loses.

KEY SCRIPTURES

- 1 John 2:1
- 1 Timothy 2:5
- Romans 8:34
- Hebrews 12:24
- Genesis 4:10
- Hebrews 7:25
- Hebrews 4:16

CHAPTER 5

THE ROLE OF THE HOLY SPIRIT AS WITNESS

E very courtroom requires witnesses—those who testify to truth, confirm evidence, and establish credibility in a case. In the courtroom of heaven, the Holy Spirit serves as a divine Witness. He testifies to the truth of Christ, to the believer's adoption as children of God, and to the power of the gospel in their lives.

THE SPIRIT BEARS WITNESS WITH OUR SPIRIT

Paul writes:

> **"The Spirit itself beareth witness with our spirit, that we are the children of God." (Romans 8:16, KJV).**

This means that when the accuser rises to question our identity, the Holy Spirit testifies on our behalf. His witness confirms that we belong to God, silencing the lies of the enemy.

THE WITNESS OF CONVICTION

Jesus explained the Spirit's role in the world as one who convicts and testifies:

> **"And when he is come, he will reprove the world of sin, and of righteousness, and of judgment." (John 16:8, KJV).**

> **"Howbeit when he, the Spirit of truth, is come, he will guide you into all truth… and he will shew you things to come. He shall glorify me." (John 16:13–14, KJV).**

Here the Spirit acts as a witness of truth. He exposes sin, confirms righteousness, and testifies of the inevitable judgment. In court terms, He provides the evidence that no one can deny.

THE SPIRIT CONFIRMS THE WORD OF CHRIST

John declared:

> **"This is he that came by water and blood, even Jesus Christ… and it is the Spirit that beareth witness, because the Spirit is truth." (1 John 5:6, KJV).**

The Holy Spirit testifies to the truth of Christ's work on the cross. He validates the evidence of the blood, confirming that it is sufficient for the redemption of humanity.

THE WITNESS OF POWER

The Spirit also bears witness through demonstrations of God's power. Paul said:

"And my speech and my preaching was not with enticing words of man's wisdom, but in demonstration of the Spirit and of power." (1 Corinthians 2:4, KJV).

Miracles, signs, and wonders are not only acts of compassion—they are testimonies in the courtroom of heaven that Jesus is Lord and that His gospel is true.

THE SPIRIT AS COMFORTING WITNESS

In the midst of accusations, the Holy Spirit not only testifies to heaven but also reassures the believer's heart. Jesus called Him the Comforter (Parakletos), the One who stands beside us.

"But the Comforter, which is the Holy Ghost, whom the Father will send in my name, he shall teach you all things, and bring all things to your remembrance." (John 14:26, KJV).

When Satan tries to overwhelm us with guilt and fear, the Spirit reminds us of God's promises, bearing witness that we are forgiven, justified, and loved.

THE TWOFOLD WITNESS

In earthly courts, the testimony of two or three witnesses establishes a matter (**see Deuteronomy 19:15**). In the heavenly courtroom, we see a powerful agreement:

1. Jesus, our Advocate, speaks for us.

2. The Holy Spirit testifies within us.

Together, their voices cannot be overturned. Heaven's case for the believer is secured by the strongest possible witness stand.

APPLICATION: LIVING BY THE SPIRIT'S TESTIMONY

When believers grasp the Spirit's role as witness, they can:

- Reject doubt about their salvation (**see Romans 8:16**).

- Walk confidently in truth, not confusion (**see John 16:13**).

- Stand bold in faith, knowing the Spirit confirms Christ's work (**see 1 John 5:6**).

The next time accusations come, remember: the Spirit of God Himself rises as a witness in your defense. His testimony is unshakable because He is truth.

KEY SCRIPTURES

- Romans 8:16
- John 16:8, 13–14
- 1 John 5:6
- 1 Corinthians 2:4
- John 14:26
- Deuteronomy 19:15

PART II

THE PROCEEDINGS OF HEAVEN'S COURT

CHAPTER 6

THE BOOKS ARE OPENED: RECORDS AND EVIDENCE

Every courtroom requires evidence. No case is complete without records, documents, and testimonies that reveal the truth. In the courtroom of heaven, scripture shows that books are opened before the Judge. These books contain the records of every person's life—their deeds, words, motives, and decisions. Nothing is hidden from the all-seeing eye of God.

THE VISION OF DANIEL

The prophet Daniel was given a glimpse of this courtroom scene:

> **"I beheld till the thrones were cast down, and the Ancient of days did sit, whose garment was white as snow… the judgment was set, and the books were opened." (Daniel 7:9–10, KJV).**

This reveals two powerful truths:

1. **Judgment is not random**—it is based on documented evidence.

2. **The Judge does not forget**—every record is preserved until the appointed time.

THE BOOKS AT THE FINAL JUDGMENT

John also saw this scene in the Book of Revelation:

> **"And I saw the dead, small and great, stand before God; and the books were opened: and another book was opened, which is the book of life: and the dead were judged out of those things which were written in the books, according to their works." (Revelation 20:12, KJV).**

There are at least two categories of books:

1. **The Books of Records** – detailing the works of men, both righteous and wicked.

2. **The Book of Life** – containing the names of those redeemed by the blood of the Lamb.

The first set reveals evidence of human conduct. The second reveals whether the person has accepted the saving work of Christ.

NOTHING IS HIDDEN

Jesus made it clear that nothing escapes the record-keeping of heaven:

> **"For there is nothing covered, that shall not be revealed; neither hid, that shall not be known." (Luke 12:2, KJV).**

"But I say unto you, That every idle word that men shall speak, they shall give account thereof in the day of judgment." (Matthew 12:36, KJV).

Every word, action, and thought becomes evidence in the courtroom of heaven. What is whispered in secret is recorded as faithfully as what is proclaimed in public.

THE RIGHTEOUS JUDGE REVIEWS THE EVIDENCE

God does not judge based on rumors, assumptions, or false testimony. He judges on the accurate record of every life.

"For God shall bring every work into judgment, with every secret thing, whether it be good, or whether it be evil." (Ecclesiastes 12:14, KJV).

"But after thy hardness and impenitent heart treasurest up unto thyself wrath against the day of wrath and revelation of the righteous judgment of God." (Romans 2:5, KJV).

This assures us that His verdicts are always just—because they are based on undeniable evidence.

THE CASE OF THE BELIEVER

For the believer, the records of sin have been wiped clean by the blood of Jesus.

"Blotting out the handwriting of ordinances that was against us, which was contrary to us, and took it out of the way, nailing it to his cross." (Colossians 2:14, KJV).

This means that when our "case file" is presented in court, the charges once written against us are no longer there. What the Judge sees is the righteousness of Christ applied to our lives.

APPLICATION: LIVING WITH ETERNITY IN VIEW

Knowing that our lives are recorded in heaven should impact how we live on earth. We must:

- Walk carefully, knowing every deed is written down (**see Ephesians 5:15**).

- Guard our words, as they are evidence in court (**see Matthew 12:36**).

- Rejoice that our names are written in the Book of Life (**see Luke 10:20**).

When the books are opened, the believer stands confident—not in personal perfection, but in Christ's redemption.

KEY SCRIPTURES

- Daniel 7:9–10
- Revelation 20:12
- Luke 12:2
- Matthew 12:36
- Ecclesiastes 12:14
- Romans 2:5
- Colossians 2:14
- Luke 10:20

CHAPTER 7

TESTIMONIES AND SPIRITUAL WITNESSES

In a courtroom, after evidence is presented, witnesses are often called to testify. Their role is to confirm the truth, provide credibility, and strengthen the case. In the heavenly courtroom, spiritual witnesses rise to testify on behalf of God's Word, His people, and His covenant. Their voices echo throughout scripture, showing that heaven's judgments are never without confirmation.

THE TESTIMONY OF TWO OR THREE WITNESSES

The principle of witnesses is rooted in God's law:

> **"At the mouth of two witnesses, or three witnesses, shall he that is worthy of death be put to death; but at the mouth of one witness he shall not be put to death." (Deuteronomy 17:6, KJV).**

God Himself established that no matter could be settled without adequate testimony. This principle still holds in the heavenly courtroom. The enemy may accuse, but God always raises a testimony against the accusations.

THE WITNESS OF THE WORD

The scriptures themselves serve as witnesses. Jesus declared:

"Search the scriptures; for in them ye think ye have eternal life: and they are they which testify of me." (John 5:39, KJV).

The Word of God testifies in our favor, declaring promises, covenant rights, and the finished work of Christ. When believers declare the Word in prayer, they are calling the written witness to testify in court.

THE WITNESS OF THE BLOOD

The blood of Jesus also rises as a witness.

"...and to the blood of sprinkling, that speaketh better things than that of Abel." (Hebrews 12:24, KJV).

Abel's blood cried out for vengeance (**see Genesis 4:10**), but the blood of Jesus testifies for mercy and forgiveness. In the heavenly courtroom, the blood is undeniable evidence and a powerful witness that the price has been paid.

THE WITNESS OF THE SPIRIT

The Holy Spirit also testifies, not only in heaven but within us.

"The Spirit itself beareth witness with our spirit, that we are the children of God." (Romans 8:16, KJV).

"…It is the Spirit that beareth witness, because the Spirit is truth." (1 John 5:6, KJV).

When accusations come, the Spirit rises as a divine witness to confirm that we belong to God and that Christ's work is complete.

THE WITNESS OF THE SAINTS

There is also a great "cloud of witnesses" who testify by their lives and faith.

"Wherefore seeing we also are compassed about with so great a cloud of witnesses, let us lay aside every weight, and the sin which doth so easily beset us, and let us run with patience the race that is set before us." (Hebrews 12:1, KJV).

The testimonies of Abraham, Moses, David, Paul, and countless others stand in the courtroom as living evidence that faith in God's promises is never in vain. Their lives testify that the Judge is righteous, the Advocate is faithful, and the accuser is defeated.

THE WITNESS OF OUR TESTIMONY

Finally, believers themselves are called to bear witness.

"And they overcame him by the blood of the Lamb, and by the word of their testimony." (Revelation 12:11, KJV).

Our testimony is not just personal—it is legal evidence. When we declare what God has done, it becomes part of the courtroom record, silencing the enemy and glorifying Christ.

APPLICATION: CALLING THE WITNESSES

In prayer, believers can "call their witnesses":

- Declare the Word of God as testimony.
- Plead the blood of Jesus as legal evidence.
- Acknowledge the Spirit's witness within.
- Stand in agreement with the testimonies of the saints.
- Speak boldly of personal testimony as proof of God's power.

When these voices are raised, the believer's case cannot be overturned. Heaven rules in favor of the redeemed.

KEY SCRIPTURES

- Deuteronomy 17:6
- John 5:39
- Hebrews 12:24
- Genesis 4:10
- Romans 8:16
- 1 John 5:6
- Hebrews 12:1
- Revelation 12:11

CHAPTER 8

THE POWER OF THE BLOOD AS LEGAL EVIDENCE

In every courtroom, the strength of a case rests upon the evidence presented. In the courtroom of heaven, no evidence carries more weight, more authority, or more finality than the blood of Jesus Christ. His blood is not just a symbol of sacrifice—it is legal evidence that eternally cancels the accusations of the enemy and secures the believer's freedom.

THE BLOOD: HEAVEN'S SUPREME EVIDENCE

When Jesus died on the cross, His blood was shed not only for forgiveness but also as legal proof of redemption. The writer of Hebrews declares:

> **"Neither by the blood of goats and calves, but by his own blood he entered in once into the holy place, having obtained eternal redemption for us." (Hebrews 9:12, KJV).**

Unlike the blood of Old Testament sacrifices, which served only as temporary coverings, the blood of Jesus permanently satisfies the demands of divine justice. It is heaven's undeniable exhibit that sin has been paid for in full.

THE BLOOD THAT SPEAKS

The blood of Jesus is not silent—it testifies continually before the throne of God.

> **"…and to the blood of sprinkling, that speaketh better things than that of Abel." (Hebrews 12:24, KJV).**

Abel's blood cried for justice (**see Genesis 4:10**), but Jesus' blood speaks of mercy, forgiveness, and reconciliation. Every time the accuser rises to bring charges, the blood of Jesus speaks louder, silencing his voice.

THE BLOOD AS CLEANSING EVIDENCE

One of the strongest legal powers of the blood is its ability to cleanse.

> **"But if we walk in the light, as he is in the light… the blood of Jesus Christ his Son cleanseth us from all sin." (1 John 1:7, KJV).**

> **"In whom we have redemption through his blood, the forgiveness of sins, according to the riches of his grace." (Ephesians 1:7, KJV).**

In court terms, this means the evidence of guilt is wiped away. The handwriting of ordinances that stood against us is erased by the blood (**see Colossians 2:14**). What once condemned us no longer exists in the heavenly records.

THE BLOOD AS JUSTIFYING EVIDENCE

Paul explained the legal standing the believer receives through the blood:

> **"Much more then, being now justified by his blood, we shall be saved from wrath through him." (Romans 5:9, KJV).**

Justification is a legal term meaning to be declared righteous. Through the blood, the Judge pronounces a verdict of "Not Guilty" over every believer.

THE BLOOD GRANTS ACCESS

The blood not only removes guilt but also grants believers the legal right to enter God's presence.

> **"Having therefore, brethren, boldness to enter into the holiest by the blood of Jesus." (Hebrews 10:19, KJV).**

In court language, the blood grants us access to the throne room. We no longer stand at a distance—through the blood, we are welcomed to present our petitions directly before the Judge.

OVERCOMING BY THE BLOOD

The Book of Revelation shows that the blood is not only past evidence but also present power in spiritual warfare:

> **"And they overcame him by the blood of the Lamb, and by the word of their testimony." (Revelation 12:11, KJV).**

The blood is the believer's greatest weapon against the accusations of Satan. It disarms the adversary and ensures that no legal ground remains for his charges.

APPLICATION: PLEADING THE BLOOD

To "plead the blood" in prayer is to present it as evidence in the courtroom of heaven. It is not a ritualistic phrase but a legal declaration:

- That sin has been paid for.
- That guilt has been removed.
- That access has been granted.
- That the accuser has been silenced.

When the believer pleads the blood, they align their case with heaven's most powerful evidence.

KEY SCRIPTURES

- Hebrews 9:12
- Hebrews 12:24
- Genesis 4:10
- 1 John 1:7
- Ephesians 1:7
- Colossians 2:14
- Romans 5:9
- Hebrews 10:19
- Revelation 12:11

CHAPTER 9

OVERCOMING BY THE WORD OF OUR TESTIMONY

In the courtroom of heaven, the blood of Jesus is the supreme evidence, but it is joined by another powerful element—the word of our testimony. Scripture reveals that the believer's spoken testimony is not just a story; it is legal proof in the heavenly court that God's Word is true, that Christ's work is real, and that the accuser has been defeated.

THE HEAVENLY VERDICT OF OVERCOMERS

John records in Revelation:

> **"And they overcame him by the blood of the Lamb, and by the word of their testimony; and they loved not their lives unto the death." (Revelation 12:11, KJV).**

Notice the twofold strategy of victory:

1. **The Blood of the Lamb** – God's evidence.

2. **The Word of Testimony** – The believer's evidence.

The blood provides the legal grounds; the testimony provides the confirming witness. Together, they seal the case in favor of the saints.

THE POWER OF TESTIMONY IN COURT

In earthly courtrooms, a testimony is sworn evidence. It carries weight and can determine the outcome of a case. In the heavenly courtroom, our testimony affirms agreement with what the blood has already accomplished.

> **"...this is the victory that overcometh the world, even our faith." (1 John 5:4, KJV).**

> **"For with the heart man believeth unto righteousness; and with the mouth confession is made unto salvation." (Romans 10:10, KJV).**

Faith in the heart must be joined with confession by the mouth. When we speak God's Word and declare His works, our testimony becomes legal proof of our faith.

THE TESTIMONY OF DELIVERANCE

Testimony is not only about salvation—it includes declaring how God has delivered us from sin, bondage, or affliction.

> **"I will speak of thy testimonies also before kings, and will not be ashamed." (Psalm 119:46, KJV).**

> **"Come and hear, all ye that fear God, and I will declare what he hath done for my soul." (Psalm 66:16, KJV).**

Each declaration reinforces the record of heaven and exposes the lies of the accuser.

THE TESTIMONY OF JESUS

At the center of every testimony is Christ Himself.

> **"...for the testimony of Jesus is the spirit of prophecy." (Revelation 19:10, KJV).**

This means that our testimony is not just about personal experiences—it is about what Jesus has done in us and through us. When we speak of His power, our words carry prophetic weight, declaring His victory in the present reality.

TESTIMONY AND THE CLOUD OF WITNESSES

Hebrews reminds us that the lives of those who have gone before serve as enduring testimonies:

> **"Wherefore seeing we also are compassed about with so great a cloud of witnesses..." (Hebrews 12:1, KJV).**

Their testimonies inspire us to run faithfully, and our testimonies become part of that eternal record, adding to heaven's witness stand.

APPLICATION: SPEAKING AS A WITNESS

Every believer has a testimony. Some may seem dramatic, others simple, but each carries legal weight in heaven when aligned with the blood of Jesus. To testify is to:

- Declare God's promises aloud.
- Share personal experiences of His grace.
- Speak the Word with boldness in prayer.
- Prophesy the finished work of Christ over circumstances.

When we testify, we are not merely encouraging others—we are strengthening our case in the heavenly courtroom.

KEY SCRIPTURES

- Revelation 12:11
- 1 John 5:4
- Romans 10:10
- Psalm 119:46
- Psalm 66:16
- Revelation 19:10
- Hebrews 12:1

CHAPTER 10

ANGELIC ACTIVITY IN THE COURTROOM

Every courtroom has attendants—bailiffs, officers, and record keepers who maintain order and carry out the Judge's instructions. In the heavenly courtroom, this role is filled by angels. They are not idle spectators; they are active participants in the legal proceedings of heaven, ensuring that God's decrees are executed on earth as they are in heaven.

ANGELS SURROUND THE THRONE

The prophet Daniel gave us a glimpse of the courtroom filled with angelic beings:

> **"A fiery stream issued and came forth from before him: thousand thousands ministered unto him, and ten thousand times ten thousand stood before him: the judgment was set, and the books were opened." (Daniel 7:10, KJV).**

Here, the Judge sits, the books are opened, and myriads of angels stand in attendance—a heavenly court staff prepared to serve at His command.

ANGELS AS MINISTERS OF JUSTICE

The psalmist declared:

> **"Bless the LORD, ye his angels, that excel in strength, that do his commandments, hearkening unto the voice of his word." (Psalm 103:20, KJV).**

In the courtroom, when the Judge issues a verdict, the angels execute it. They enforce the Word of God, making sure that heaven's decisions are carried out on the earth.

ANGELS AS MESSENGERS OF JUDGMENT

Throughout scripture, angels are dispatched to execute judgments and deliver messages of divine justice:

- An angel shut the mouths of lions in Daniel's trial (**see Daniel 6:22**).

- Angels struck down Sodom with destruction (**see Genesis 19:13**).

- An angel smote Herod when he refused to give glory to God (**see Acts 12:23**).

In each case, angels carried out the verdict of heaven's courtroom.

ANGELS AS GUARDIANS OF THE RIGHTEOUS

Angels are not only enforcers of judgment but also defenders of the saints.

"The angel of the LORD encampeth round about them that fear him, and delivereth them." (Psalm 34:7, KJV).

"For he shall give his angels charge over thee, to keep thee in all thy ways." (Psalm 91:11, KJV).

In court language, angels act as protective officers—ensuring that no unlawful attack of the enemy can prosper against those under the Judge's protection.

ANGELS OBSERVE THE COURTROOM

Paul reminds us that angels are also witnesses to God's dealings with His people:

"...for we are made a spectacle unto the world, and to angels, and to men." (1 Corinthians 4:9, KJV).

They behold the unfolding of heaven's justice and rejoice when God's verdict favors His saints.

APPLICATION: PARTNERING WITH ANGELS IN PRAYER

While we do not command angels by our own authority, our prayers aligned with God's Word activate their ministry. When we speak God's decrees, angels are dispatched to enforce them.

"Are they not all ministering spirits, sent forth to minister for them who shall be heirs of salvation?" (Hebrews 1:14, KJV).

This means every believer has heavenly officers attending their case. When accusations rise, angels enforce the Advocate's defense, protect the believer, and carry out heaven's verdict.

KEY SCRIPTURES

- Daniel 7:10
- Psalm 103:20
- Daniel 6:22
- Genesis 19:13
- Acts 12:23
- Psalm 34:7
- Psalm 91:11
- 1 Corinthians 4:9
- Hebrews 1:14

PART III

VERDICTS AND JUDGMENTS

CHAPTER 11

RIGHTEOUS VERDICTS FROM THE THRONE

In every courtroom, after evidence is presented and testimonies are given, the most important moment arrives—the Judge renders a verdict. In the heavenly courtroom, this is when God, the Righteous Judge, declares His decision. These verdicts carry eternal weight because they are based on His unchanging Word, His perfect justice, and His holy nature.

THE THRONE OF RIGHTEOUS JUDGMENT

The psalmist declares:

> **"But the LORD shall endure for ever: he hath prepared his throne for judgment. And he shall judge the world in righteousness, he shall minister judgment to the people in uprightness." (Psalm 9:7–8, KJV).**

God's throne is not only a seat of power but also of judgment. Unlike human judges, who may err or be swayed by bribes or corruption, God's verdicts are always just, impartial, and final.

THE JUDGE RULES IN FAVOR OF HIS PEOPLE

Daniel gives a remarkable vision of God's courtroom:

> **"I beheld, and the same horn made war with the saints, and prevailed against them; until the Ancient of days came, and judgment was given to the saints of the most High; and the time came that the saints possessed the kingdom." (Daniel 7:21–22, KJV).**

This shows that the saints do not always appear victorious in earthly battles. But when the heavenly court issues its verdict, the tide turns. The Judge rules in favor of His people, and authority is restored to them.

GOD'S VERDICT SILENCES THE ACCUSER

Once the Judge speaks, the accuser has no further argument.

> **"Who shall lay any thing to the charge of God's elect? It is God that justifieth." (Romans 8:33, KJV).**

Satan may accuse, but God's verdict of justification overrules every charge. The word "justify" is a legal term, meaning the Judge has declared us righteous and acquitted of all guilt.

THE VERDICT OF MERCY OVER JUDGMENT

Even when evidence of guilt is undeniable, the blood of Jesus gives the Judge the legal right to extend mercy.

> **"...mercy rejoiceth against judgment." (James 2:13, KJV).**

This means that for the believer, God's verdict is not condemnation but mercy, because Christ has borne the penalty in our place.

VERDICTS THAT ESTABLISH DESTINY

God's verdicts do more than dismiss charges—they also establish destiny.

> **"Thou shalt also decree a thing, and it shall be established unto thee: and the light shall shine upon thy ways." (Job 22:28, KJV).**

When heaven rules in our favor, doors open, breakthroughs come, and destinies unfold. His decrees release blessings, assignments, and kingdom authority into the earth.

FINAL VERDICTS CANNOT BE APPEALED

In earthly courts, verdicts can be appealed to higher courts. But in heaven, there is no higher court to overrule God.

> **"For the LORD is our judge, the LORD is our lawgiver, the LORD is our king; he will save us." (Isaiah 33:22, KJV).**

The Judge, the Lawgiver, and the King are one. His verdict is supreme, unquestionable, and eternal.

APPLICATION: STANDING ON HEAVEN'S VERDICT

As believers, we must learn to stand on the verdicts of heaven. When God declares us justified, we must silence the voice of condemnation. When He decrees mercy, we must reject fear. When He rules in favor of our destiny, we must walk boldly into it.

The verdict has already been declared: **"There is therefore now no condemnation to them which are in Christ Jesus." (Romans 8:1, KJV).**

KEY SCRIPTURES

- Psalm 9:7–8
- Daniel 7:21–22
- Romans 8:33
- James 2:13
- Job 22:28
- Isaiah 33:22
- Romans 8:1

CHAPTER 12

THE SENTENCE OF THE WICKED

E very courtroom not only delivers acquittals for the innocent but also sentences for the guilty. In the heavenly courtroom, God—the Righteous Judge—will pronounce unchangeable judgment on Satan, his demons, and all unrepentant sinners. The same throne that grants mercy to the redeemed issues wrath upon the rebellious.

THE CERTAINTY OF THE WICKED'S SENTENCE

The Bible assures us that the wicked will not escape divine justice:

"For the LORD knoweth the way of the righteous: but the way of the ungodly shall perish." (Psalm 1:6, KJV).

Unlike human courts, where criminals sometimes escape due to lack of evidence or flawed systems, the heavenly court is flawless. Nothing escapes the Judge's eye, and no sin goes unpunished unless covered by the blood of Jesus.

SATAN'S FINAL SENTENCE

The devil, the great accuser, already has his eternal sentence sealed.

> **"And the devil that deceived them was cast into the lake of fire and brimstone, where the beast and the false prophet are, and shall be tormented day and night for ever and ever." (Revelation 20:10, KJV).**

This is the ultimate verdict against the adversary: eternal torment with no possibility of parole. His fate is already written, and his accusations cannot change his destiny.

THE SENTENCE OF FALLEN ANGELS

The demons who followed Satan's rebellion will also face judgment:

> **"And the angels which kept not their first estate, but left their own habitation, he hath reserved in everlasting chains under darkness unto the judgment of the great day." (Jude 1:6, KJV).**

Their sentence is imprisonment and eternal chains, awaiting the final judgment. No demonic power will escape God's justice.

THE SENTENCE OF THE UNREPENTANT

The same courtroom that offers mercy through Christ will also sentence those who reject Him.

> **"And whosoever was not found written in the book of life was cast into the lake of fire." (Revelation 20:15, KJV).**

"The wicked shall be turned into hell, and all the nations that forget God." (Psalm 9:17, KJV).

For the unrepentant, the sentence is eternal separation from God. This sobering reality should compel every believer to preach the gospel with urgency.

THE GRADATION OF JUDGMENT

The Bible also teaches that judgment is measured according to knowledge and deeds.

"And that servant, which knew his lord's will, and prepared not himself... shall be beaten with many stripes. But he that knew not... shall be beaten with few stripes." (Luke 12:47–48, KJV).

This reveals the fairness of the Judge. Sentences will reflect the measure of rebellion and rejection of God's truth.

THE JUSTICE OF THE JUDGE

Some may question why eternal punishment is necessary, but scripture affirms the justice of God's sentences:

"For the righteous LORD loveth righteousness; his countenance doth behold the upright." (Psalm 11:7, KJV).

"Seeing it is a righteous thing with God to recompense tribulation to them that trouble you." (2 Thessalonians 1:6, KJV).

The Judge's holiness demands justice. To ignore sin would compromise His righteousness. The sentence of the wicked is not cruelty—it is justice.

APPLICATION: LIVING IN THE FEAR OF GOD

The reality of eternal sentencing should stir us to:

- Live holy, knowing God's justice is unchanging.
- Walk humbly, remembering it is mercy that saved us.
- Preach urgently, to rescue the lost from eternal judgment.

The wicked may prosper for a season on earth, but heaven's court will have the final word.

KEY SCRIPTURES

- Psalm 1:6
- Revelation 20:10
- Jude 1:6
- Revelation 20:15
- Psalm 9:17
- Luke 12:47–48
- Psalm 11:7
- 2 Thessalonians 1:6

CHAPTER 13

THE REWARDS OF THE RIGHTEOUS

Just as the guilty receive their sentence, the faithful receive their reward. The heavenly courtroom is not only a place of judgment but also a place of reward, where God honors those who loved, served, and obeyed Him on earth.

THE RIGHTEOUS JUDGE REWARDS FAITHFULNESS

Paul confidently declared:

> **"Henceforth there is laid up for me a crown of righteousness, which the Lord, the righteous judge, shall give me at that day: and not to me only, but unto all them also that love his appearing." (2 Timothy 4:8, KJV).**

Notice that Paul saw his reward as certain, not because of his own strength, but because the righteous Judge had decreed it. What the Judge promises, He fulfills.

CROWNS FOR THE FAITHFUL

The Bible describes several crowns that believers may receive as eternal rewards:

1. **The Crown of Life** – For those who endure trials faithfully and remain steadfast even unto death.

    > **"Blessed is the man that endureth temptation: for when he is tried, he shall receive the crown of life." (James 1:12, KJV).**

Also called the "martyr's crown" (**see Revelation 2:10**).

2. **The Incorruptible Crown** – For those who discipline themselves in the Christian race.

    > **"Now they do it to obtain a corruptible crown; but we an incorruptible." (1 Corinthians 9:25, KJV).**

3. **The Crown of Righteousness** – For those who eagerly await Christ's return.

    > **"Henceforth there is laid up for me a crown of righteousness, which the Lord, the righteous judge, shall give me at that day: and not to me only, but unto all them also that love his appearing." (2 Timothy 4:8, KJV).**

4. **The Crown of Glory** – For faithful pastors, shepherds, and leaders who serve God's flock with humility.

"And when the chief Shepherd shall appear, ye shall receive a crown of glory that fadeth not away." (1 Peter 5:4, KJV).

5. **The Crown of Rejoicing** – Also known as the soul-winner's crown.

    "For what is our hope, or joy, or crown of rejoicing? Are not even ye in the presence of our Lord Jesus Christ at his coming?" (1 Thessalonians 2:19, KJV).

Each crown represents not earthly glory but eternal honor granted by the Judge Himself.

REWARDS ACCORDING TO WORKS

The rewards of the righteous are based on how faithfully they served the Lord.

"For the Son of man shall come in the glory of his Father with his angels; and then he shall reward every man according to his works." (Matthew 16:27, KJV).

"For God is not unrighteous to forget your work and labour of love, which ye have shewed toward his name." (Hebrews 6:10, KJV).

While salvation is by grace, rewards are by works. Our deeds done for Christ on earth echo in eternity.

INHERITANCE OF THE SAINTS

The righteous are also given an inheritance that cannot be corrupted or taken away.

> **"To an inheritance incorruptible, and undefiled, and that fadeth not away, reserved in heaven for you." (1 Peter 1:4, KJV).**

This inheritance includes eternal life, ruling with Christ, and access to the fullness of His glory.

ETERNAL COMMENDATION

The greatest reward of all will be hearing the words of the Master:

> **"Well done, thou good and faithful servant: thou hast been faithful over a few things, I will make thee ruler over many things: enter thou into the joy of thy lord." (Matthew 25:21, KJV).**

These words are the ultimate verdict in favor of the righteous.

APPLICATION: LIVING FOR ETERNAL REWARDS

Understanding the rewards of the righteous should shape our lives today. We must:

- Serve faithfully, even when unseen.
- Endure trials with perseverance.
- Love Christ's appearing and live in readiness.
- Win souls, knowing they will be our eternal crown of rejoicing.

The Judge will not forget—even the smallest act of obedience will be rewarded.

KEY SCRIPTURES

- 2 Timothy 4:8
- James 1:12
- Revelation 2:10
- 1 Corinthians 9:25
- 1 Peter 5:4
- 1 Thessalonians 2:19
- Matthew 16:27
- Hebrews 6:10
- 1 Peter 1:4
- Matthew 25:21

CHAPTER 14

WHEN HEAVEN OVERRULES EARTHLY DECREES

In earthly life, men and institutions pass judgments—sometimes unjust, sometimes oppressive. Yet in the heavenly courtroom, the decrees of God hold supreme authority. When heaven speaks, no earthly law, no demonic decree, and no human opposition can stand against it.

THE SUPREME AUTHORITY OF HEAVEN

The psalmist affirms the supremacy of God's Word:

"Forever, O LORD, thy word is settled in heaven." (Psalm 119:89, KJV).

What is settled in heaven cannot be unsettled on earth. When God issues a decree, it overrides every human judgment. His Word is the highest constitution, and His courtroom is the ultimate appellate court.

BIBLICAL EXAMPLES OF HEAVEN'S OVERRULE

1. **Daniel in the Lions' Den**

   Earthly decree: No man shall pray to any god but the king (**see Daniel 6:7–9**).

   Heaven's overrule: God sent His angel and shut the lions' mouths (**see Daniel 6:22**).

2. **The Three Hebrew Boys in the Furnace**

   Earthly decree: Bow to the golden image or be cast into the fiery furnace (**see Daniel 3:6**).

   Heaven's overrule: The fire had no power, and the Son of God walked with them (**see Daniel 3:25–27**).

3. **Peter's Imprisonment**

   Earthly decree: Herod's verdict was execution (**see Acts 12:4–6**).

   Heaven's overrule: An angel of the Lord opened the prison doors and set him free (**see Acts 12:7–11**).

These examples show that when heaven issues its ruling, the decrees of kings, rulers, and oppressors are nullified.

HEAVEN OVERRULES SATANIC DECREES

Satan often tries to write death sentences over lives through sickness, curses, or bondage. But Jesus cancels every decree of the enemy.

> **"Blotting out the handwriting of ordinances that was against us, which was contrary to us, and took it out of the way, nailing it to his cross." (Colossians 2:14, KJV).**

The cross is heaven's legal cancellation stamp over every curse and accusation written against us.

HEAVEN OVERRULES HUMAN CONDEMNATION

Men may reject, condemn, or label us, but God's verdict stands above theirs.

> **"It is God that justifieth. Who is he that condemneth?" (Romans 8:33–34, KJV).**

> **"No weapon that is formed against thee shall prosper; and every tongue that shall rise against thee in judgment thou shalt condemn." (Isaiah 54:17, KJV).**

When God declares us justified, no earthly condemnation can hold us captive.

HEAVEN OVERRULES NATURAL LIMITATIONS

Even natural laws and impossibilities bow to heaven's decrees. Sarah was barren, but God decreed fruitfulness **(see Genesis 21:1–2)**. Lazarus was dead, but Jesus decreed life **(see John 11:43–44)**.

This means that when heaven speaks, even biology, science, and history must submit to His Word.

APPLICATION: STANDING ON HEAVEN'S DECREES

As believers, we must learn to appeal to the highest court of heaven when faced with the decrees of men.

- When sickness speaks death, declare God's decree of healing (**see Isaiah 53:5**).

- When fear whispers defeat, declare His decree of victory (**see 1 Corinthians 15:57**).

- When rejection tries to define you, declare His decree of adoption (**see Romans 8:15**).

Earthly rulings may carry weight, but heaven's verdict is final.

KEY SCRIPTURES

- Psalm 119:89
- Daniel 6:22
- Daniel 3:25–27
- Acts 12:7–11
- Colossians 2:14
- Romans 8:33–34
- Isaiah 54:17
- Genesis 21:1–2
- John 11:43–44
- Isaiah 53:5
- 1 Corinthians 15:57

- Romans 8:15

CHAPTER 15

THE FINAL JUDGMENT SEAT
OF CHRIST

The courtroom of heaven will one day reach its ultimate climax. Every soul—great or small, righteous or wicked—will stand before the throne of God. In that moment, all arguments will cease, all appeals will be over, and the Judge will render eternal verdicts.

THE TWO ETERNAL JUDGMENTS

The Bible reveals two distinct judgments in the final courtroom sessions:

1. The Judgment Seat of Christ (for believers):

    "For we must all appear before the judgment seat of Christ; that every one may receive the things done in his body, according to that he hath done, whether it be good or bad." (2 Corinthians 5:10, KJV).

This judgment is not about salvation—it is about rewards. Believers will give an account of their works and receive crowns or suffer loss of reward (**see 1 Corinthians 3:13–15**).

2. The Great White Throne Judgment (for unbelievers):

> **"And I saw a great white throne, and him that sat on it… and the dead were judged out of those things which were written in the books, according to their works." (Revelation 20:11–12, KJV).**

This judgment is a final condemnation for all whose names are not written in the Book of Life (**see Revelation 20:15**).

THE JUDGE ON THE THRONE

John describes the majesty of this moment:

> **"And I saw a great white throne, and him that sat on it, from whose face the earth and the heaven fled away." (Revelation 20:11, KJV).**

This is the ultimate court session. The Judge is not a man, not a system, but Almighty God Himself—before whom creation trembles.

BOOKS AND RECORDS REVIEWED

Once again, the evidence is presented:

"...and the books were opened: and another book was opened, which is the book of life." (Revelation 20:12, KJV).

The books of deeds, the Book of Life, and heaven's records are all consulted. Nothing is overlooked; every secret is revealed.

REWARDS FOR THE RIGHTEOUS

For the faithful in Christ, the Judge will reward according to faithfulness.

"And, behold, I come quickly; and my reward is with me, to give every man according as his work shall be." (Revelation 22:12, KJV).

"And when the chief Shepherd shall appear, ye shall receive a crown of glory that fadeth not away." (1 Peter 5:4, KJV).

This is the joy of the believer—to stand before Christ, not in fear of condemnation, but in anticipation of commendation.

CONDEMNATION FOR THE WICKED

For the unrepentant, the sentence is eternal separation:

"And whosoever was not found written in the book of life was cast into the lake of fire." (Revelation 20:15, KJV).

"...the Lord Jesus shall be revealed from heaven with his mighty angels, in flaming fire taking vengeance on them that know not God." (2 Thessalonians 1:7–8, KJV).

The wicked may escape earthly justice, but they will not escape the final judgment.

NO APPEAL BEYOND THIS COURT

In earthly systems, a verdict may be appealed to a higher court. But in the final judgment, there is no higher authority to appeal to.

> **"For we must all appear before the judgment seat of Christ…" (2 Corinthians 5:10, KJV).**

The Judge's word is final, and His ruling is eternal.

APPLICATION: LIVING WITH THE FINAL JUDGMENT IN MIND

The reality of the final courtroom should inspire us to live with urgency and holiness:

- To keep our names in the Book of Life through faith in Christ.

- To serve faithfully, knowing our labor is not in vain (**see 1 Corinthians 15:58**).

- To evangelize urgently, warning others of the coming judgment.

Every thought, word, and action is heading toward this ultimate courtroom. The wise prepare now, for tomorrow may be too late.

KEY SCRIPTURES

- 2 Corinthians 5:10
- 1 Corinthians 3:13–15
- Revelation 20:11–12, 15
- Revelation 22:12
- 1 Peter 5:4
- 2 Thessalonians 1:7–8
- 1 Corinthians 15:58

PART IV

WALKING IN VICTORY AFTER THE VERDICT

CHAPTER 16

HOW TO PRESENT YOUR CASE BEFORE GOD

In every courtroom, cases must be presented before the Judge. Lawyers study the law, prepare their arguments, and bring forth evidence to support their claims. In the heavenly courtroom, believers also have the privilege of presenting their petitions before God, appealing to His justice, His Word, and the blood of Jesus Christ.

THE INVITATION TO PRESENT OUR CASE

God Himself invites His people to bring their case before Him:

> **"Put me in remembrance: let us plead together: declare thou, that thou mayest be justified." (Isaiah 43:26, KJV).**

The Judge of all the earth asks us to remind Him of His promises, to plead our case according to His Word, and to declare our legal standing in Christ. This is not arrogance—it is bold obedience to His invitation.

THE PATTERN OF BIBLICAL PLEADING

1. **Abraham – Intercession for Sodom.** Abraham pleaded with God on the basis of His justice:

   "Shall not the Judge of all the earth do right?" (Genesis 18:25, KJV).

Abraham appealed to God's character, not his own merit.

2. **Hezekiah – Appeal for Healing.** King Hezekiah, facing death, presented his case:

   "Remember now, O LORD, I beseech thee, how I have walked before thee in truth and with a perfect heart." (Isaiah 38:3, KJV).

God heard and extended his life by fifteen years.

3. **Moses – Intercession for Israel.** Moses appealed to God's covenant and reputation among the nations:

   "Wherefore should the Egyptians speak, and say, For mischief did he bring them out…? Turn from thy fierce wrath, and repent of this evil against thy people." (Exodus 32:12, KJV).

God relented and spared Israel because Moses pleaded the covenant.

THE LEGAL BASIS OF OUR CASE

When we present our case, it must be grounded on:

- **The Word of God** – God cannot deny His own Word (**see Numbers 23:19**).

- **The Blood of Jesus** – Our ultimate evidence of justification (**see Hebrews 9:14**).

- **The Covenant Promises** – God honors His covenant forever (**see Psalm 89:34**).

Earthly courts may accept flawed arguments, but heaven only responds to truth, covenant, and the cross.

PRACTICAL STEPS IN PRESENTING YOUR CASE

1. **Acknowledge the Judge's Authority.** Begin by honoring God as the righteous Judge (**see Psalm 75:7**).

2. **Confess and Repent of Sin.** Remove any legal ground the enemy might use (**see 1 John 1:9**).

3. **Present Evidence from Scripture.** Declare God's promises as legal grounds for your request (**see Isaiah 55:11**).

4. **Plead the Blood of Jesus.** Present the blood as the final proof of redemption (**see Revelation 12:11**).

5. **Call Witnesses to Testify.** Bring in the Word, the Spirit, and your testimony as supporting evidence.

6. **Make Your Petition Boldly.**

> **"Let us therefore come boldly unto the throne of grace, that we may obtain mercy, and find grace to help in time of need." (Hebrews 4:16, KJV).**

THE POWER OF LEGAL PRAYER

Praying in the language of the courtroom is different from begging. It is petitioning the Judge with confidence in His Word. When we say, **"Father, Your Word declares…"**, we are presenting legal evidence. When we plead the blood, we are offering irrefutable proof. When we testify of His goodness, we are submitting witness statements.

APPLICATION: LIVING AS KINGDOM PETITIONERS

Every believer is not just a child of God but also a legal petitioner in His courtroom. We must stop approaching prayer as powerless pleading and begin presenting our case as rightful heirs of the covenant.

When believers present their case correctly, heaven responds with verdicts of healing, deliverance, provision, and victory.

KEY SCRIPTURES

- Isaiah 43:26
- Genesis 18:25
- Isaiah 38:3
- Exodus 32:12
- Numbers 23:19

- Psalm 89:34
- Psalm 75:7
- 1 John 1:9
- Isaiah 55:11
- Revelation 12:11
- Hebrews 4:16

CHAPTER 17

PRAYERS THAT MOVE THE JUDGE

In every courtroom, not all arguments carry the same weight. Some are weak and easily dismissed, while others are strong and persuasive. In the heavenly courtroom, the prayers of God's people can be weak (lacking faith, alignment, or substance), or they can be powerful, bold, and rooted in the Word of God. The Bible reveals the kinds of prayers that move the Judge of all the earth to act.

PRAYER THAT APPEALS TO GOD'S COVENANT

Moses prayed on the basis of God's covenant promises, and God relented from destroying Israel:

> **"Remember Abraham, Isaac, and Israel, thy servants, to whom thou swarest by thine own self, and saidst unto them, I will multiply your seed…" (Exodus 32:13, KJV).**

Covenant prayers remind God of His sworn promises. Since He cannot lie (**see Numbers 23:19**), such prayers carry undeniable weight in the courtroom of heaven.

PRAYER THAT APPEALS TO GOD'S CHARACTER

Abraham interceded for Sodom, not based on merit, but on God's justice:

> **"Shall not the Judge of all the earth do right?" (Genesis 18:25, KJV).**

When we appeal to God's holiness, righteousness, love, or mercy, we are aligning our petitions with His very nature—something He cannot deny.

PRAYER THAT IS BOLD AND PERSISTENT

Jesus taught that persistence in prayer matters:

> **"And shall not God avenge his own elect, which cry day and night unto him…? I tell you that he will avenge them speedily." (Luke 18:7–8, KJV).**

Just as a persistent widow wore down an unjust judge, persistent prayer demonstrates unwavering faith that moves the righteous Judge to act.

PRAYER THAT IS BASED ON THE WORD

Prayers that quote God's Word are powerful because His Word is the highest law of the courtroom.

> **"So shall my word be that goeth forth out of my mouth: it shall not return unto me void." (Isaiah 55:11, KJV).**

**"...thou hast magnified thy word above all thy name."
(Psalm 138:2, KJV).**

When we pray scripture, we are essentially presenting God's own laws back to Him. Such prayers cannot be overturned.

PRAYER THAT IS BACKED BY THE BLOOD

The blood of Jesus gives legal authority to our prayers.

> **"Having therefore, brethren, boldness to enter into the holiest by the blood of Jesus." (Hebrews 10:19, KJV).**

When we pray "through the blood," we present the most powerful evidence heaven recognizes. The Judge must honor it, for it is the legal payment for our redemption.

PRAYER OF THE RIGHTEOUS

God responds to the prayers of those walking in righteousness:

> **"The effectual fervent prayer of a righteous man availeth much." (James 5:16, KJV).**

Holiness strengthens our case, while unrepented sin weakens it. This is why confession and repentance always precede powerful intercession.

PRAYER THAT IS OFFERED IN FAITH

Faith-filled prayers move heaven's court, while doubt-filled prayers falter.

"But let him ask in faith, nothing wavering... For let not that man think that he shall receive any thing of the Lord." (James 1:6–7, KJV).

Faith is the spiritual "currency" of the courtroom. Without it, no case can stand.

APPLICATION: HOW TO PRAY COURTROOM PRAYERS

To pray prayers that move the Judge, we must:

1. Ground them in the Word of God.
2. Base them on the blood of Jesus.
3. Appeal to His character and covenant.
4. Pray with persistence, boldness, and faith.
5. Live with a righteous heart, free from unrepented sin.

When we pray this way, our petitions do not fall to the ground. They rise before the throne as undeniable legal cases, and the Judge responds with rulings in our favor.

KEY SCRIPTURES

- Exodus 32:13
- Numbers 23:19
- Genesis 18:25
- Luke 18:7–8
- Isaiah 55:11
- Psalm 138:2
- Hebrews 10:19
- James 5:16

- James 1:6–7

CHAPTER 18

BREAKING LEGAL RIGHTS OF THE ENEMY

In every courtroom, the accuser builds his case by finding legal grounds to charge the defendant. Satan operates the same way in the heavenly courtroom. He cannot simply accuse without cause; he seeks entry points through sin, disobedience, or generational iniquities. To walk in full victory, believers must break the enemy's legal rights through the blood of Jesus and repentance.

THE ENEMY SEEKS LEGAL GROUNDS

The devil is called the accuser of the brethren (**see Revelation 12:10**). His accusations are not baseless; they are often tied to areas where people have given him access.

"Neither give place to the devil." (Ephesians 4:27, KJV).

"Place" here means legal foothold. Unforgiveness, unrepented sin, and disobedience become open doors for the enemy's accusations.

EXAMPLES OF LEGAL GROUNDS IN SCRIPTURE

1. Unrepented Sin

> **"He that covereth his sins shall not prosper: but whoso confesseth and forsaketh them shall have mercy." (Proverbs 28:13, KJV).**

Sin gives the enemy a voice in court until it is confessed and forsaken.

2. Generational Curses

> **"...visiting the iniquity of the fathers upon the children unto the third and fourth generation." (Exodus 20:5, KJV).**

Patterns of sin in families can serve as legal grounds if not broken by the blood of Christ.

3. Wrong Covenants or Agreements

Israel suffered when they made a covenant with the Gibeonites without consulting God (**see Joshua 9:14–20**).

Ungodly agreements or spiritual covenants create legal access points for the enemy.

4. **Unforgiveness**

> **"But if ye forgive not men their trespasses, neither will your Father forgive your trespasses." (Matthew 6:15, KJV).**

Unforgiveness gives the enemy a strong legal case against us.

HOW TO BREAK THE ENEMY'S LEGAL RIGHTS

1. **Repentance and Confession**

> **"If we confess our sins, he is faithful and just to forgive us our sins, and to cleanse us from all unrighteousness." (1 John 1:9, KJV).**

Confession removes the legal ground of unrepented sin.

2. **Renouncing Ungodly Agreements**

Verbally break and renounce every covenant not made with God.

> **"Through thy precepts I get understanding: therefore I hate every false way." (Psalm 119:104, KJV).**

3. **Pleading the Blood**

Present the blood of Jesus as irrefutable evidence that the debt is paid.

"...the blood of Jesus Christ his Son cleanseth us from all sin." (1 John 1:7, KJV).

4. Forgiving Others

Release forgiveness to shut the door of accusation.

"...forgive, and ye shall be forgiven." (Luke 6:37, KJV).

5. Declaring God's Verdict

Speak God's justification over your life.

"Who shall lay any thing to the charge of God's elect? It is God that justifieth." (Romans 8:33, KJV).

APPLICATION: LIVING FREE FROM LEGAL CLAIMS

Breaking the legal rights of the enemy is not a one-time act but a lifestyle. Daily repentance, walking in holiness, and living by the Spirit ensure the accuser has no foothold.

When the enemy comes to accuse, believers can stand boldly and declare: *"The case against me has been dismissed by the blood of Jesus."*

KEY SCRIPTURES

- Revelation 12:10
- Ephesians 4:27

- Proverbs 28:13
- Exodus 20:5
- Joshua 9:14–20
- Matthew 6:15
- 1 John 1:9
- Psalm 119:104
- 1 John 1:7
- Luke 6:37
- Romans 8:33

CHAPTER 19

HOW TO ENFORCE HEAVEN'S VERDICTS ON EARTH

In every courtroom, when a judge issues a ruling, it must be enforced. A verdict without enforcement has no effect. In the heavenly courtroom, God has already ruled in favor of His children through the blood of Jesus Christ. The responsibility of believers is to enforce those rulings on earth by faith, prayer, and spiritual authority.

HEAVEN'S VERDICT MUST BE ENFORCED

Jesus taught His disciples to pray:

> **"Thy kingdom come, Thy will be done in earth, as it is in heaven." (Matthew 6:10, KJV).**

This is courtroom language. God's will is already decreed in heaven, but believers must enforce that verdict in the earth realm.

THE ROLE OF THE BELIEVER IN ENFORCEMENT

God issues the verdict, but the believer enforces it by exercising dominion:

> **"Behold, I give unto you power to tread on serpents and scorpions, and over all the power of the enemy: and nothing shall by any means hurt you." (Luke 10:19, KJV).**

> **"Whatsoever ye shall bind on earth shall be bound in heaven: and whatsoever ye shall loose on earth shall be loosed in heaven." (Matthew 18:18, KJV).**

This shows the dual responsibility: heaven decrees, earth enforces.

HOW HEAVEN'S VERDICTS ARE ENFORCED

1. **Through Decrees and Declarations**

> **"Thou shalt also decree a thing, and it shall be established unto thee: and the light shall shine upon thy ways." (Job 22:28, KJV).**

Believers enforce verdicts by declaring God's Word over their lives, families, and nations.

2. **Through Persistent Prayer**

> **"...the kingdom of heaven suffereth violence, and the violent take it by force." (Matthew 11:12, KJV).**

114

Courtroom rulings are enforced through prayer that refuses to let go until the manifestation comes.

3. Through Spiritual Warfare

> **"For the weapons of our warfare are not carnal, but mighty through God to the pulling down of strong holds." (2 Corinthians 10:4, KJV).**

Enforcement sometimes requires resisting demonic opposition that seeks to delay or block heaven's decrees.

4. Through Angelic Assistance

> **"Bless the LORD, ye his angels... that do his commandments, hearkening unto the voice of his word." (Psalm 103:20, KJV).**

Angels enforce God's Word when believers declare it in alignment with heaven.

5. Through Lifestyle of Faith and Obedience

Living in obedience to God ensures that nothing hinders the verdict from manifesting.

> **"If ye be willing and obedient, ye shall eat the good of the land." (Isaiah 1:19, KJV).**

BIBLICAL EXAMPLES OF ENFORCEMENT

- Elijah declared heaven's verdict of drought and later its end, and it manifested (**see 1 Kings 17:1; 18:41**).

- Joshua enforced God's judgment on Jericho through obedience and prophetic action (**see Joshua 6:20**).

- The Apostles enforced Christ's rulings by casting out demons, healing the sick, and proclaiming liberty (**see Mark 16:17–18**).

Each case shows that verdicts must be spoken, acted upon, and enforced.

APPLICATION: BECOMING HEAVEN'S ENFORCERS

As believers, we are not passive recipients of God's rulings—we are kingdom enforcers. Every prayer, every declaration, every act of faith is part of enforcing heaven's verdicts on earth.

When the Judge declares healing, we enforce it through faith-filled confession and action.

When He declares freedom, we enforce it by rejecting bondage.

When He declares blessing, we enforce it by walking in obedience.

Heaven has ruled. Now we must enforce.

KEY SCRIPTURES

- Matthew 6:10
- Luke 10:19

- Matthew 18:18
- Job 22:28
- Matthew 11:12
- 2 Corinthians 10:4
- Psalm 103:20
- Isaiah 1:19
- 1 Kings 17:1; 18:41
- Joshua 6:20
- Mark 16:17–18

CHAPTER 20

LIVING WITH THE
AWARENESS OF THE
COURTROOM

To live with courtroom awareness means to constantly remember that we are part of a divine legal system. God is the Judge, Christ is our Advocate, the Spirit is our Witness, angels are court officers, and Satan is the accuser. Every day, choices are recorded, words are weighed, and petitions are filed. When believers live in this reality, they walk more carefully, more boldly, and more victoriously.

LIVING CAREFULLY – KNOWING EVERYTHING IS RECORDED

Jesus warned:

> **"But I say unto you, That every idle word that men shall speak, they shall give account thereof in the day of judgment." (Matthew 12:36, KJV).**

Every word, thought, and action is evidence in the heavenly court. Living with this awareness makes us careful not to give the enemy ammunition through careless speech or hidden sin.

LIVING BOLDLY – KNOWING THE CASE IS IN OUR FAVOR

Paul wrote: **"If God be for us, who can be against us?" (Romans 8:31, KJV).**

In the courtroom of heaven, the verdict has already been rendered in favor of the redeemed. Believers can live boldly, knowing the Advocate is interceding and the Judge has justified them.

LIVING WATCHFULLY – KNOWING THE ACCUSER IS ACTIVE

Revelation describes Satan as: **"…the accuser of our brethren… which accused them before our God day and night." (Revelation 12:10, KJV).**

Awareness of the courtroom reminds us to stay spiritually alert. Satan is relentless in searching for legal grounds, but we can live watchfully by keeping doors closed through repentance, forgiveness, and obedience.

LIVING PRAYERFULLY – BRINGING CASES BEFORE GOD DAILY

Daniel modeled this awareness by praying three times a day despite opposition **(see Daniel 6:10)**. His prayers were not empty rituals; they were petitions filed daily before the heavenly court. Believers today enforce verdicts and keep their case strong through constant prayer and declaration of the Word.

LIVING FAITHFULLY – AWAITING THE FINAL VERDICT

Paul declared: **"Henceforth there is laid up for me a crown of righteousness, which the Lord, the righteous judge, shall give me at that day…" (2 Timothy 4:8, KJV).**

Courtroom awareness keeps us faithful until the end, knowing the Judge will reward those who endure.

DAILY PRACTICES OF COURTROOM AWARENESS

1. **Examine Yourself Regularly** – Close any legal doors the enemy may try to exploit (**see 2 Corinthians 13:5**).

2. **Guard Your Words** – Speak life, not death (**see Proverbs 18:21**).

3. **Keep Records Clean** – Repent quickly when you stumble (**see 1 John 1:9**).

4. **File Petitions in Prayer** – Present your case often, using scripture and the blood as evidence.

5. **Walk in Boldness** – Live as one who already has heaven's verdict in their favor (**see Romans 8:37**).

APPLICATION: LIVING AS HEAVEN'S CITIZENS ON EARTH

Living with courtroom awareness means walking daily as one under divine order. You live knowing heaven is watching, recording, and ruling, but also defending, justifying, and rewarding. It's a life of reverence, vigilance, and victory.

KEY SCRIPTURES

- Matthew 12:36
- Romans 8:31
- Revelation 12:10
- Daniel 6:10
- 2 Timothy 4:8
- 2 Corinthians 13:5
- Proverbs 18:21
- 1 John 1:9
- Romans 8:37

CHAPTER 21

WORSHIP AS COURTROOM PROTOCOL

In every earthly courtroom, there is order, reverence, and respect. No one barges into a judge's presence casually; everyone rises when the judge enters, and only those permitted may speak. In the heavenly courtroom, worship is the protocol by which we approach the Judge. It honors His authority, aligns our hearts, and positions us to receive His verdicts.

WORSHIP ACKNOWLEDGES GOD AS JUDGE

The psalmist declared:

> **"Give unto the LORD the glory due unto his name; worship the LORD in the beauty of holiness." (Psalm 29:2, KJV).**

Worship is not optional—it is due. Just as a court officer honors the authority of the judge, worship acknowledges God's supreme authority in the courtroom of heaven.

WORSHIP INVITES THE PRESENCE OF THE JUDGE

When worship rises, the Judge takes His seat in the court.

> **"But thou art holy, O thou that inhabitest the praises of Israel." (Psalm 22:3, KJV).**

This means worship is not only protocol—it is an invitation for God to dwell among His people and preside over their case.

WORSHIP SILENCES THE ACCUSER

When worship is lifted, the enemy's voice is silenced.

> **"Out of the mouth of babes and sucklings hast thou ordained strength because of thine enemies, that thou mightest still the enemy and the avenger." (Psalm 8:2, KJV).**

Worship functions as legal order in the courtroom—it shuts down the accusations of Satan and shifts the atmosphere toward heaven's favor.

WORSHIP ALIGNS US WITH HEAVEN'S COURTROOM

Heaven itself is full of worship. John saw the throne surrounded with continual praise:

> **"And the four beasts... rest not day and night, saying, Holy, holy, holy, Lord God Almighty, which was, and is, and is to come." (Revelation 4:8, KJV).**

When we worship, we align ourselves with the eternal rhythm of heaven's court, where worship is the constant sound.

WORSHIP PRECEDES VERDICTS AND DELIVERANCE

Throughout scripture, worship unlocked rulings and breakthroughs:

- **Jehoshaphat's Army:** They worshiped, and God overruled their enemies (**see 2 Chronicles 20:22**).

- **Paul and Silas in Prison:** They worshiped, and the court of heaven issued a verdict of deliverance (**see Acts 16:25–26**).

- **Hannah:** She worshiped after presenting her petition, and God ruled in her favor (**see 1 Samuel 1:19**).

In each case, worship was the courtroom protocol that moved heaven to act.

APPLICATION: PRACTICING WORSHIP AS PROTOCOL

1. **Begin Every Petition with Worship** – Honor the Judge before presenting your case (**see Psalm 100:4**).

2. **Use Worship to Silence Accusations** – When the enemy condemns you, lift your voice in praise.

3. **Worship in Spirit and Truth** – (**see John 4:24**) – True worship is sincere and aligns with God's Word.

4. **Let Worship Seal Your Case** – End petitions with thanksgiving and adoration, as though the verdict is already won.

When we honor the Judge with worship, we enter His court in the right posture—humble, reverent, and confident.

KEY SCRIPTURES

- Psalm 29:2
- Psalm 22:3
- Psalm 8:2
- Revelation 4:8
- 2 Chronicles 20:22
- Acts 16:25–26
- 1 Samuel 1:19
- Psalm 100:4
- John 4:24

CHAPTER 23

LIVING AS A VICTORIOUS WITNESS

In the courtroom of heaven, witnesses play a crucial role. They testify to the truth, confirm the evidence, and silence false accusations. Believers are called to live as living witnesses—not only speaking of Christ's victory but embodying it daily so that both heaven and earth recognize the reality of our redemption.

OUR LIVES ARE TESTIMONIES

Paul reminded the Corinthians:

"Ye are our epistle written in our hearts, known and read of all men." (2 Corinthians 3:2, KJV).

This means our lives are like written testimonies—open evidence of God's power and grace. Even when we are silent, how we live becomes evidence in the heavenly courtroom and before the world.

THE WITNESS OF TRANSFORMATION

One of the most undeniable forms of testimony is a changed life.

> **"Therefore if any man be in Christ, he is a new creature: old things are passed away; behold, all things are become new." (2 Corinthians 5:17, KJV).**

Transformation is living proof that heaven's verdict has been rendered in our favor. It is evidence that cannot be dismissed by the accuser.

THE WITNESS OF ENDURANCE

When believers remain faithful in trials, they testify louder than any sermon.

> **"Wherefore seeing we also are compassed about with so great a cloud of witnesses, let us lay aside every weight… and let us run with patience the race that is set before us." (Hebrews 12:1, KJV).**

Our endurance in suffering is courtroom evidence that Christ is greater than the enemy's schemes.

THE WITNESS OF GOOD WORKS

Jesus declared:

> **"Let your light so shine before men, that they may see your good works, and glorify your Father which is in heaven." (Matthew 5:16, KJV).**

Good works are not for salvation, but they serve as public testimony that heaven has justified us. They glorify the Judge and silence the accuser.

THE WITNESS OF BOLD CONFESSION

The believer is also called to testify openly about Christ:

> **"Whosoever therefore shall confess me before men, him will I confess also before my Father which is in heaven." (Matthew 10:32, KJV).**

Confession is courtroom language. When we confess Christ, our testimony is submitted in heaven's record, and Jesus affirms it before the Father.

LIVING AS OVERCOMERS

Revelation reminds us:

> **"And they overcame him by the blood of the Lamb, and by the word of their testimony." (Revelation 12:11, KJV).**

Victory in the courtroom is not just about words spoken in prayer, but about living in such a way that our entire life becomes a testimony of God's grace.

APPLICATION: BECOMING A LIVING WITNESS

1. **Walk in Integrity** – Let your conduct be consistent with your confession (**see Proverbs 11:3**).

2. **Endure Trials with Faith** – Turn hardship into testimony of God's sustaining power.

3. **Serve Others Boldly** – Let your works shine as evidence of Christ's life in you.

4. **Confess Christ Daily** – Do not hide your faith—declare Jesus openly in word and deed.

When we live as victorious witnesses, our lives become irrefutable evidence that Christ is alive, Satan is defeated, and heaven's courtroom has ruled in our favor.

KEY SCRIPTURES

- 2 Corinthians 3:2
- 2 Corinthians 5:17
- Hebrews 12:1
- Matthew 5:16
- Matthew 10:32
- Revelation 12:11
- Proverbs 11:3

CHAPTER 24

THE ETERNAL COURTROOM AND THE LAMB'S BOOK OF LIFE

In every courtroom, records are kept—legal documents, verdicts, and registries. In the heavenly courtroom, the greatest record of all is the Lamb's Book of Life. This book contains the names of all who have been redeemed by the blood of Jesus Christ. In the final judgment, this book will serve as the ultimate evidence of who belongs to the kingdom and who does not.

THE EXISTENCE OF THE BOOK

John records in Revelation:

> **"And whosoever was not found written in the book of life was cast into the lake of fire." (Revelation 20:15, KJV).**

This book is not symbolic—it is real. It is the final registry of heaven's citizens. Entry into this book is not by works, status, or heritage, but solely by the new birth through Christ.

THE BOOK BELONGS TO THE LAMB

It is called the Lamb's Book of Life because it belongs to Jesus, the Lamb who was slain.

> **"And all that dwell upon the earth shall worship him, whose names are not written in the book of life of the Lamb slain from the foundation of the world." (Revelation 13:8, KJV).**

The Judge entrusted the record to the Son, for He purchased redemption with His blood.

NAMES WRITTEN FROM THE FOUNDATION OF THE WORLD

God, in His sovereignty, knew from the beginning those who would respond to His call.

> **"According as he hath chosen us in him before the foundation of the world…" (Ephesians 1:4, KJV).**

Yet, the writing of names is also tied to personal faith and acceptance of Christ. Salvation is a gift, but receiving it is each person's responsibility.

THE POSSIBILITY OF BLOTTING OUT NAMES

The Bible warns that names can be removed from the book if one turns away.

> **"And the LORD said unto Moses, Whosoever hath
> sinned against me, him will I blot out of my book."
> (Exodus 32:33, KJV).**

> **"He that overcometh, the same shall be clothed in white
> raiment; and I will not blot out his name out of the book
> of life…" (Revelation 3:5, KJV).**

This means perseverance in faith and holiness is essential. To reject
Christ or turn away is to risk eternal erasure from the register.

THE BOOK OF REMEMBRANCE

Alongside the Book of Life, Malachi speaks of another heavenly
record:

> **"Then they that feared the LORD spake often one to
> another: and the LORD hearkened, and heard it, and a
> book of remembrance was written before him for them
> that feared the LORD, and that thought upon his name."
> (Malachi 3:16, KJV).**

This shows that God records not only salvation but also
faithfulness, words, and works—all of which will be remembered
in the courtroom of eternity.

THE FINAL COURTROOM CHECK

At the Great White Throne, books will be opened—including the
Book of Life.

> **"And I saw the dead, small and great, stand before God;
> and the books were opened: and another book was**

opened, which is the book of life…" (Revelation 20:12, KJV).

No argument, no excuse, no appeal will matter if a name is absent. The Judge will check the registry, and that alone will determine eternal destiny.

APPLICATION: ENSURING YOUR NAME IS WRITTEN

The most urgent reality of the heavenly courtroom is this: *Is your name written in the Lamb's Book of Life?*

- Receive Christ by faith (**see John 1:12**).
- Walk in obedience and holiness (**see Hebrews 12:14**).
- Endure to the end (**see Matthew 24:13**).

Living with courtroom awareness means living daily with the assurance that your name is sealed in the book.

KEY SCRIPTURES

- Revelation 20:15
- Revelation 13:8
- Ephesians 1:4
- Exodus 32:33
- Revelation 3:5
- Malachi 3:16
- Revelation 20:12
- John 1:12
- Hebrews 12:14
- Matthew 24:13

CHAPTER 25

VICTORY IN THE COURTROOM OF HEAVEN

The heavenly courtroom is not designed to leave God's children trembling in uncertainty. It is the place where victory is secured, righteousness is established, and the believer's destiny is affirmed. Through the blood of Jesus, the accusations of Satan are silenced, the verdict is declared, and we walk as overcomers in Christ.

THE VERDICT HAS ALREADY BEEN RENDERED

The believer does not fight for victory but from victory.

"There is therefore now no condemnation to them which are in Christ Jesus, who walk not after the flesh, but after the Spirit." (Romans 8:1, KJV).

The Judge has already ruled in favor of the redeemed. Condemnation has been dismissed, the case is closed, and the accuser has lost his standing.

THE ADVOCATE GUARANTEES OUR TRIUMPH

Jesus' continual intercession ensures the verdict stands.

> **"Who is he that condemneth? It is Christ that died, yea rather, that is risen again, who is even at the right hand of God, who also maketh intercession for us." (Romans 8:34, KJV).**

This means the Advocate never loses a case, and His defense cannot fail.

THE BLOOD SECURES THE VICTORY

The blood of Jesus is the eternal evidence that ensures we prevail.

> **"And they overcame him by the blood of the Lamb, and by the word of their testimony; and they loved not their lives unto the death." (Revelation 12:11, KJV).**

The blood is our legal foundation; our testimony is our declaration; our surrender seals the case.

THE JUDGE DECLARES US MORE THAN CONQUERORS

Paul triumphantly concludes:

> **"Nay, in all these things we are more than conquerors through him that loved us." (Romans 8:37, KJV).**

Not just conquerors, but more than conquerors. This means the victory is not marginal—it is overwhelming, undeniable, and eternal.

LIVING IN DAILY VICTORY

To walk in courtroom victory means:

1. **Refusing Condemnation** – Do not accept guilt when the Judge has acquitted you (**see Romans 8:33**).

2. **Walking in Boldness** – Approach the throne with confidence (**see Hebrews 4:16**).

3. **Declaring the Verdict** – Speak God's rulings into your life, family, and ministry (**see Job 22:28**).

4. **Resisting the Accuser** – Enforce the verdict by rejecting lies and standing firm (**see James 4:7**).

5. **Rejoicing in the Outcome** – Worship the Judge who has rendered the final verdict in your favor (**see Psalm 149:5–9**).

ETERNAL VICTORY AWAITS

The final courtroom scene ends not with despair, but with eternal triumph. The righteous will hear:

"Well done, thou good and faithful servant... enter thou into the joy of thy lord." (Matthew 25:21, KJV).

This is the eternal confirmation of heaven's ruling—forever justified, forever victorious, forever in the presence of the Judge.

APPLICATION: LIVING AS A VICTORIOUS BELIEVER

The courtroom of heaven teaches us that:

- The accuser has no lasting claim.
- The Advocate never loses.
- The Judge always rules righteously.
- The verdict has already been declared in our favor.

Therefore, we live, pray, worship, and declare from the place of victory—not hoping for it, but walking in it.

KEY SCRIPTURES

- Romans 8:1
- Romans 8:34
- Revelation 12:11
- Romans 8:37
- Romans 8:33
- Hebrews 4:16
- Job 22:28
- James 4:7
- Psalm 149:5–9
- Matthew 25:21

CONCLUSION

LIVING IN THE LIGHT OF HEAVEN'S COURTROOM

The journey through the courtroom of heaven has revealed a reality both sobering and empowering. We have seen the Judge on His throne, the Accuser at work, the Advocate interceding, the Witness testifying, the evidence presented, and the verdicts delivered. We have watched as the wicked were sentenced, the righteous rewarded, and the Lamb's Book of Life opened.

But this is not merely theology to be admired—it is truth to be lived. The courtroom of heaven is active right now, and every believer has a role to play.

THE REALITY OF THE COURTROOM

Every word, every action, every choice is recorded. Heaven's books are open, and the scales of justice are perfect. Nothing is hidden from the Judge. But this reality should not bring fear—it should bring holy reverence and daily vigilance.

THE TRIUMPH OF THE BELIEVER

The good news is that the verdict has already been declared:

"Who shall lay any thing to the charge of God's elect? It is God that justifieth." (Romans 8:33, KJV).

Through the cross of Christ, the case against us has been dismissed. The blood speaks louder than the accuser. The Advocate never loses. The Judge always rules in righteousness.

THE CALL TO WALK IN VICTORY

Because the verdict has been rendered in our favor, we must live differently:

- **With Boldness** – coming before the throne without fear (**see Hebrews 4:16**).

- **With Holiness** – closing every legal door the enemy might use (**see 1 Peter 1:16**).

- **With Worship** – honoring the Judge daily with reverence (**see Psalm 29:2**).

- **With Declarations** – enforcing heaven's verdicts through our words (**see Job 22:28**).

- **With Urgency** – proclaiming the gospel, warning others of the final judgment (**see Mark 16:15**).

THE ETERNAL COURTROOM AWAITS

One day, the final session will be held. The books will be opened, and the Lamb's Book of Life will be checked. The righteous will receive their eternal inheritance, and the wicked will face eternal sentence.

But until that day, we live as victorious witnesses—testifying by our words, our lives, and our endurance that Christ reigns and the accuser is defeated.

PROPHETIC CHARGE

Beloved of God, rise up and walk in courtroom awareness. Do not live as though the enemy still has a case against you. The blood has spoken. The Advocate has won. The Judge has ruled. Now live as an enforcer of heaven's decrees—bringing His will to earth through prayer, worship, and declaration.

Let your life be an ongoing testimony that silences the accuser and magnifies the Righteous Judge. And when the final gavel strikes, may you hear the words:

> **"Well done, thou good and faithful servant... enter thou into the joy of thy Lord." (Matthew 25:21, KJV).**

This is the ultimate verdict. This is the eternal victory.

KEY SCRIPTURES

- Romans 8:33
- Hebrews 4:16
- 1 Peter 1:16

- Psalm 29:2
- Job 22:28
- Mark 16:15
- Matthew 25:21

SCRIPTURE REFERENCE INDEX

THE JUDGE OF ALL THE EARTH

- Genesis 18:25
- Psalm 75:7
- Psalm 11:7
- Romans 14:10
- Revelation 20:11

THE ACCUSER

- Revelation 12:10
- Zechariah 3:1
- Job 1:9–11
- Ephesians 4:27

THE ADVOCATE (JESUS CHRIST)

- 1 John 2:1
- Romans 8:34
- Hebrews 7:25
- Hebrews 9:24

THE WITNESS (HOLY SPIRIT & TESTIMONY)

- John 15:26
- Romans 8:16

- Revelation 12:11
- Hebrews 12:1

THE EVIDENCE IN COURT

- Daniel 7:10
- Revelation 20:12
- Malachi 3:16
- Matthew 12:36

THE VERDICTS AND SENTENCES

- Romans 8:1
- John 5:24
- Revelation 20:15
- Psalm 9:17
- 2 Thessalonians 1:6–8

REWARDS OF THE RIGHTEOUS

- 2 Timothy 4:8
- James 1:12
- 1 Peter 5:4
- 1 Thessalonians 2:19
- 1 Corinthians 9:25
- Revelation 22:12

OVERRULING EARTHLY DECREES

- Psalm 119:89
- Daniel 6:22
- Daniel 3:25–27

- Acts 12:7–11
- Colossians 2:14
- Isaiah 54:17

PRESENTING YOUR CASE

- Isaiah 43:26
- Exodus 32:12–13
- Genesis 18:25
- Isaiah 38:3
- Hebrews 4:16

BREAKING LEGAL RIGHTS OF THE ENEMY

- Proverbs 28:13
- Exodus 20:5
- Matthew 6:15
- 1 John 1:7, 9
- Romans 8:33

ENFORCING HEAVEN'S VERDICTS

- Matthew 6:10
- Luke 10:19
- Matthew 18:18
- Job 22:28
- 2 Corinthians 10:4
- Psalm 103:20

WORSHIP AS PROTOCOL

- Psalm 29:2

- Psalm 22:3
- Psalm 8:2
- Revelation 4:8
- Acts 16:25–26

DECLARATIONS THAT SHIFT ATMOSPHERES

- Proverbs 18:21
- Isaiah 55:11
- Job 22:28
- John 8:36
- 1 Peter 2:24
- Philippians 4:19
- Romans 8:37

THE LAMB'S BOOK OF LIFE

- Revelation 20:12, 15
- Revelation 13:8
- Revelation 3:5
- Exodus 32:33
- Ephesians 1:4
- Malachi 3:16

LIVING IN VICTORY

- Romans 8:1
- Romans 8:34, 37
- Revelation 12:11
- Hebrews 4:16
- James 4:7
- Matthew 25:21

www.ingramcontent.com/pod-product-compliance
Lightning Source LLC
LaVergne TN
LVHW021503080426
835509LV00018B/2385